HOW TO Write A WINNING PERSONAL STATEMENT

for Graduate and Professional School

HOW TO *Write* A WINNING PERSONAL STATEMENT

for Graduate and Professional School

Richard J. Stelzer

90-2441

Peterson's Guides
Princeton, New Jersey

**Library of Congress
Cataloging-in-Publication Data**

Stelzer, Richard J., 1949–
  How to write a winning personal statement for
graduate and professional school / Richard J.
Stelzer.

    p.   cm.

ISBN 0-87866-786-5

  1. College applications—United States. 2.
Universities and colleges—Graduate
work—Admission. 3. Professional
education—United States—Admission. I. Title.
LB2351.52.U6S74   1989
378'.1056—dc19   88–37443
                        CIP

Composition and design by Peterson's Guides

Printed in the United States of America

10 9 8 7 6 5 4 3 2 1

CONTENTS

PREFACE

Of all the tasks you face when applying to professional or graduate school—from choosing universities to preparing for and taking standardized tests, from soliciting recommendations to having transcripts sent out—writing the personal statement(s) is among the most formidable. With the keen competition for admission to graduate schools, the personal statement or autobiographical essay often becomes a crucial element of the application package. This book provides a wide array of information and suggestions that should make preparation of your personal statement easier, less intimidating, and more successful.

At the back of this book you will find a set of exclusive, revealing interviews with a group of admissions professionals from more than two dozen of the nation's top-tiered law, business, and medical schools, as well as other selected graduate programs. With candor and clarity, these professionals disclose what they look for in personal statements, describe the mistakes applicants commonly make, and offer advice on how to make your statements as effective as possible. In conjunction with the information, exercises, and advice provided on the following pages, their comments should prove an invaluable resource to you.

Naturally, nothing in this book shall be construed as guaranteeing any applicant admission to any graduate or professional school.

INTRODUCING...YOU

A personal statement or autobiographical essay represents a graduate or professional school's first introduction or exposure to you, to the way you think, and to the way you express yourself. There might be interviews later on (for medical school applicants and some others), but for now, in the beginning of the application process, the personal statement must serve as a reflection of your personality and intellect. You must sell yourself through this statement, just as you would attempt to do in a job interview, and preparation and thought are essential.

As hard as it is to write in general, it is even more difficult to write about oneself. So don't be discouraged; everyone has problems composing these statements. If you have a friend who cranks one out in 2 hours flat with no agonizing over what he or she is writing, chances are it's not a statement that will do much to enhance the prospects for admission. The ones that are good take time. The ones that are bad can sabotage your chances for success.

The personal statements or essays required of graduate and professional school applicants fall into two major categories. There is the general, comprehensive personal statement, which allows the applicant maximum latitude in terms of what he or she writes. This is the type of statement often prepared for the Personal Comments section of the standard medical school application form. It is also the kind of statement that many law school applicants elect to write.

The second category encompasses essays that are expected to be responses to very specific questions, such as those found on business school and other graduate application forms. Here you might have less latitude in terms of the content of your essay(s), but it is still possible

1

and prudent to compose a thoughtful and persuasive response that holds the reader's interest.

No matter what type of application form you are dealing with, it is extremely important that you *read each question carefully and make every effort to understand it and respond to it.* Whatever else you choose to discuss in your essay, you must be certain to address the specific question that the application poses. Some applications are more vague or general in their instructions than others; for these it is often possible to compose almost any sort of essay you wish. In these instances, it is almost as if you are participating in the dream interview in which you both ask and answer the questions. You have virtually total control and you also have a remarkable opportunity that you can either maximize or squander. The choice is yours.

It is crucial to understand that even graduate schools offering the same degree often have very different requirements with respect to the personal statement(s). For example, there *are* some law schools that expect essays to revolve around the issue of why you wish to attend law school (or become a lawyer). Many law schools, however, very deliberately avoid asking that question because they are bored with the generally homogeneous responses it tends to provoke, or simply believe another question (or type of statement) provides them with a far more interesting and revealing look at their applicants. For the latter law schools, the applicant's motivation for studying law becomes almost a peripheral issue.

Explain Yourself

The most surprising thing about many would-be law students, M.B.A. candidates, and other professional and graduate school applicants is their failure to define in their own minds exactly who they are and why they are seeking a certain career. Admissions committee members are looking, in many instances, for interesting, thoughtful, persuasive explanations of applicants' career choices, as well as for statements that serve to reveal the applicant and add a dimension not available from other sources.

Be Specific

Therefore, two important words to keep in mind when writing your essay are: *Be specific!* Medical schools, for example, aren't too interested in hearing you express the opinion that you would make an excellent doctor unless you can back it up with specific reasons. Your decision to become a lawyer, doctor, businessman, engineer, educator, scientist (or whatever) should be *logical*, the result of specific experiences and factors. Don't keep admissions committees in the dark about your reasoning (provided the question asked makes this an appropriate topic of discussion) or about what these specific experiences and factors are. A good, general personal statement should make it easy for the reader to ascertain the origin of your interest in a profession or field and see the growth of that interest over a period of time. Your application to professional or graduate school should emerge as the logical conclusion to your story.

An Important Exercise

In order to begin writing your personal statement—your story—you'll need the answers to some basic questions. Pretend you have 5 minutes to speak with someone from an admissions committee. They ask, "What's most important

3

for us to know about you?" You must make a case for yourself and hold the listener's interest. What would you say? Figuring that out, determining what you would say, is a challenge that is critical to your success in preparing an effective statement. Answering the following questions will facilitate this task, but be patient with yourself.

Questions to Ask Yourself

- What's special, unique, distinctive, and/or impressive about you or your life story? What details of your life (personal or family problems, history, people or events that have shaped you or influenced your goals) might help the committee better understand you or help set you apart from other applicants?

- When did you originally become interested in this field and what have you since learned about it—and about yourself—that has further stimulated your interest and reinforced your conviction that you are well suited to this field? What insights have you gained?

- *How* have you learned about this field—through classes, readings, seminars, work or other experiences, or conversations with people already in the field?

- If work experiences have consumed significant periods of time during your college years, what have you learned (leadership or managerial skills, for example), and how has the work contributed to your personal growth?

- What are your career goals?

- Are there any gaps or discrepancies in your academic record that you should explain (great grades and mediocre LSAT scores, for

example, or a distinct upward pattern to GPA
if it was only average in the beginning)?

- Have you had to overcome any unusual obstacles or hardships (e.g., economic, familial,
physical) in your life?

- What personal characteristics (integrity,
compassion, persistence, for example) do you
possess that would enhance your prospects
for success in the field or profession? Is there
a way to demonstrate or document that you
have these characteristics?

- What skills (leadership, communicative, analytical, for example) do you possess?

- Why might you be a stronger candidate for
graduate school—and more successful and effective in the profession or field—than other
applicants?

- What are the most compelling reasons you
can give for the admissions committee to be
interested in you?

Answering all of these questions will not be
easy, but this is an exercise that will have great
practical benefit in readying you to write an outstanding personal statement.

Probably at least part of the answer to the
question, "What's most important for the admissions committee to know about you?" will be contained in the first paragraph of your essay. But
one thing is certain: once you complete your essay, you will know exactly what you would say in
that hypothetical meeting with the admissions
committee member. Writing the essay in the
correct way will have forced you to think about
yourself, your experiences and your goals, and to
formulate an interesting and persuasive presentation of your story.

Tell A Story

The personal statement is (in many cases) just that, a sort of story. By that I *don't* mean that you should fabricate or invent *anything*; be truthful and stick to the facts. What you should do, however, is think in terms of telling a story. *One of the worst things you can do with your personal statement is to bore the admissions committee*, yet that is exactly what most applicants do. If your statement is fresh, lively, different—not to mention articulate—you'll be putting yourself way ahead of the pack. Why? Because by distinguishing yourself through your story—by setting yourself apart from other applicants—you'll make yourself *memorable*. If the admissions committee remembers you because what you wrote was *catchy* (without being inappropriate), you have an obvious advantage; much of what is submitted to the committees is distressingly homogeneous and eminently forgettable, if not sleep-inducing.

It never hurts if the story you tell has drama. Some people have life stories that are inherently dramatic. For example, here in the United States there are many applicants who have come from other countries, often settling in a new homeland with no money, connections, or knowledge of the language or culture. Such circumstances, which obviously apply only to a minority of applicants, constitute dramatic obstacles that the applicant has had to overcome to reach his or her present position. But you do not have to be foreign-born to have experienced some sort of trauma that could be relevant, absorbing, and—if properly presented—memorably dramatic. (The latitude you have in composing your essay(s) obviously has to relate to the question or questions asked.)

Find An Angle

If you're like most people, however, your life story *lacks* drama, so figuring out a way to make it interesting becomes the big challenge. Finding an angle or "hook" is vital. For example, a law school applicant with ordinary grades but outstanding credits in other areas might choose to present herself as follows, emphasizing exceptional athletic prowess and relevant work experience in order to distinguish herself: "As a former college tennis star, now playing in the women's professional circuit, I am in a position which many athletes would covet. If I want, I can earn a living in pro sports. For most, this would be a dream come true. In my own case, however, I have decided—after working as a paralegal in a law firm—that I can make a more significant mark as an attorney, winning my battles not on tennis courts but in courts of law." This would provide an offbeat and memorable introduction to such an applicant's story.

Concentrate on Your Opening Paragraph

Keep in mind when composing your statement that the lead or opening paragraph is generally the most important. It is here that you grab the reader's attention—or lose it. Once you figure out this first paragraph, the remainder of the essay should be less problematic because you will have a framework for what you're going to say. If there's drama to your statement, it will be introduced in the opening paragraph so that the reader is eager to continue. If you're telling some sort of story, you'll use this first paragraph to introduce the elements most relevant to that story—and the ones that will hold greatest interest for the reader.

Tell What You Know

The middle section of your essay might detail your interest and experience in your particular field, as well as some of your knowledge of the field. By referring to some of what you know about a given profession, you are introducing what I call the "reality factor" into your statement. Too many people graduate from college with little or no knowledge of the nuts and bolts of the profession or field to which they aspire. In some instances they have false, glamorous ideas about being, say, a lawyer or psychologist, rather than a realistic perception of what these professions entail. Be as specific as you can in relating what you know about the field and use the language professionals use in conveying this information. Refer to experiences (work, research, etc.), classes, conversations with people in the field, books you've read, seminars you've attended, or any other sources of specific information about the career you want and why you're suited to it. If, for some reason, you don't have much specific knowledge of your future field, make it your business to do some research, and consider including what you discover in your statement.

Sometimes a personal statement can be perfectly well written in terms of language and grammar, but disastrous in lacking punch or impact and in being totally off the mark concerning what it chooses to present about the applicant. Remember, what's most important about your personal statement is *what you say* and *how you say it!* Be *selective* about what you tell the admissions committee. Often you are specifically limited to a certain number of pages (two double-spaced typed pages—or just over—should suffice for most applicants, unless multiple questions require more space), so it is necessary to pick and choose in relating your story. What you choose to say in your statement is, again, very much a reflection of *you* because it shows the committees what your priorities are, what you consider to be important. For this reason, the personal statement is often an indication, too, of your *judgment*, so be careful and give a great deal of thought to what you write. Much thinking—probably over a period of *weeks*—should, ideally, precede the writing. Think about yourself, your background, experiences and abilities—as well as what you know about the profession—and develop a strategy.

Review Your Personal History

Applicants preparing personal statements very often fail to remember or include facts (experiences, events, achievements) that are extremely relevant, either to their career choice and application or in terms of explaining what makes them tick. One law applicant almost forgot that he had spent a summer working for an assistant district attorney! And this was the most potent, relevant, and interesting "weapon" in his "arsenal"!! It sounds unbelievable but this occurs all the time. Another law school applicant almost forgot to tell the admissions committees of his experience as chief defense witness in a criminal trial. My suggestion: *review your life very carefully* (get help from family or friends, if necessary) for facets or experiences that reveal an unusual dimension, relate to your professional goals, or could serve as evidence of your suitability for a certain career. (The Preparatory Questionnaire at the back of this book will be very helpful to you.)

What Not to Include

There are certain things that normally are best left out of personal statements. In general, references to experiences or accomplishments during your high school years or earlier are not a good idea. There are exceptions, I am sure (if there was an extraordinary achievement or traumatic event that had a significant impact on your life in terms of your development or career plans, go with it), but, as a rule, introducing material from this period of your life can make your statement seem sophomoric, at a time when you *should* want to come across as a mature young adult (or as even more sophisticated if years have intervened since your undergraduate work).

Don't mention subjects that are potentially controversial; it is impossible for you to know the biases of members of various admissions committees. Religion and politics normally don't belong in these statements, although, again, there may be exceptions (an applicant who has held an important office on campus or in the community would likely want to include this fact). Personal political views usually are not appropriate for personal statements. Any views that might be interpreted as strange or highly unconventional should also be omitted because you want to avoid the possibility of offending any of the individuals in whose hands the fate of your graduate school application rests.

Sometimes there will be things you want to mention because you are proud of them, perhaps justly so. At the same time, though, there are achievements and experiences that do not belong in your statement, not because you're hiding anything but because you're being *selective* about what you write. Don't pull something out of left field—something that doesn't fit into the story you're telling or the case you're trying to build—just to stroke your own ego. Be smarter than that. Again, *be selective!*

Reviewing What's Been Said (Plus a Few New Points)

Let's review some of the points we have presented up to now, as well as a few additional thoughts (and questions) for you to consider.

- Remember that, in a general sense, what's most important is what you say and how you say it.

- Whatever else you do, be sure to answer the question(s) the admissions committee is asking.

- Determine what you would tell an admissions committee member if you had 5 minutes to answer the question "What's most important for us to know about you?" This exercise will force you to do the type of thinking that must precede the preparation of an effective personal statement. For help, refer to the list of questions you should ask yourself.

- Don't make the mistake of trying to guess what the admissions committee is looking for, and don't just write what you think the committee wants to hear. Such ploys are highly obvious to admissions people and can be detrimental to your cause.

- When appropriate, find an angle and tell a story about yourself. If your life story has drama, use it.

- You are preparing a *personal* statement. Often it is appropriate and useful to include material that is quite personal in nature.

11

- Grab the reader's attention in your opening paragraph.

- Review your life carefully—with outside help, if necessary—to make certain you're including all relevant information. (Again, see the Preparatory Questionnaire at the back of the book.)

- Be selective. Don't introduce inappropriate material or get into so much detail that your judgment can be called into question.

- Try to maintain a positive and upbeat tone. While often it is useful to deal candidly with aspects of your history that might be perceived negatively, you still want to project confidence and enthusiasm.

- Be specific when appropriate.

- Avoid potentially controversial subjects.

- Express yourself clearly and concisely.

- Adhere to stated word limits.

- Be meticulous (type and proofread your essay carefully).

- If a school wants to know why you're applying to it rather than another school, do a bit of research if necessary to find out what sets your choice apart from other universities or programs. If the school setting would provide an important geographical or cultural change for you, this might be a factor to mention.

- *Think* about what you're saying. (Is it interesting, relevant, different, memorable?)

- Be honest. Are you being yourself and revealing yourself? In many instances, admissions people are interested in finding out about who you are, and they appreciate honesty and candor. (One representative from a leading business school even told me that he likes to hear about applicants' setbacks because "through events like that, we see a lot of the qualities of rebounding. A lot of the real superstars have failed miserably at times. We think the best candidates are ones who have failed and learned from it.")

- Are you providing something more than a recitation of information available elsewhere in the application?

- Are you avoiding obvious clichés? For example, a medical school applicant who writes that he is good at science and wants to help other people is not exactly expressing an original thought. (One law school admissions representative told me, "When we discuss mistakes, we jokingly refer to the person who starts out a personal statement with a quote, either from de Tocqueville or from Shakespeare, such as the one that says, 'The first thing we do, let's kill all the lawyers.'")

- Use the Evaluative Questionnaire yourself (in addition to giving it to others) to assess the effectiveness of your rough draft.

A Word on Business School Applications

Business school applications merit special attention because, unlike most medical and law school applications, they tend to bypass the single, comprehensive personal statement in favor of multiple essays. Business schools typically require responses to at least three questions, with some schools asking for considerably more. Harvard Business School, for example, has recently been using a form with nine questions for the applicant to answer in essay form. Moreover, Harvard, in 1986, decided not to require, accept, or consider GMAT scores, a move that lends credence to speculation that substantial weight is given to the essays in determining those applicants most suitable for the HBS M.B.A. program.

Persons applying to two or more M.B.A. programs may find themselves having to formulate and compose responses to more questions than they feel they can deal with. Fortunately, there often tends to be at least some overlap in questions posed by different business schools. So while the phrasing of the question may vary from school to school, an inquiry about, for example, why the applicant has decided to seek an M.B.A. at a given school at a given time can appear on application after application. The prevalence of this particular question on so many forms would seem to suggest that the business schools are interested not only in how applicants express themselves but also in how they explain their educational and professional goals, as well as defend the merits of their candidacy for an M.B.A. program.

Certain questions on other applications are less expected, although no less challenging. For instance, several business schools offer questions concerning ethical dilemmas the applicant may have faced; some are careful to specify they do *not* want to know how the applicant acted, while other schools *do* want a description of the course of action the applicant chose to follow.

Wharton formerly asked its applicants what was surely one of the most unusual questions posed by any business school: what nine items they would choose to take along on a solo space flight and why. (In the wake of the space shuttle disaster, Wharton modified the question on 1987 applications so that it instead focused on the applicant's choices if stranded on a desert island. By 1988 the question was no longer present in any form.)

Among other questions, Stanford has requested details concerning the applicant's ideal job; the University of Michigan has asked for the applicant's assessment of the strengths and weaknesses of the M.B.A.; Harvard has been interested in alternative professions or vocations the applicant might have considered; Chicago has called for assessment and evidence of verbal and written communication skills; Yale has required that the applicant delineate his or her learning goals. UCLA formerly asked applicants to write their own essay question and answer it ("Take a risk," they advised), an approach duplicated on Kellogg's 1989 application form. Berkeley has lately asked, "What seminal influences or experiences, broadly defined, have especially contributed to your personal development?"

More common questions deal with the applicant's most significant accomplishments, events that have affected his or her growth and development, personal strengths and weaknesses, and career aspirations.

Special Advice: I mentioned earlier that it is useful to *be specific (while avoiding so much detail that you lose the reader)*. It is also important to put things into context. If you are describing your work for a certain company or institution, it is often useful to characterize that company in terms of such things as what it does and its position in the marketplace (unless, of course, it is IBM or another similarly high-profile organization). You might also want to characterize your ascension within the organization if, for example, it deviated from the usual pattern, or occurred with unusual rapidity. Also, if you are, for example, the only non-M.B.A. employee working in an environment otherwise populated exclusively by those with the M.B.A. degree, this fact might bear mentioning for a variety of reasons.

WINNING PERSONAL STATEMENTS

What you will read on the following pages are a series of successful personal essays. Notice the way in which many of the applicants have chosen an angle and told a story about themselves. In some cases they have used drama in their presentations to catch the reader's interest and set themselves apart from other applicants. When there were obstacles they had to overcome in their lives, these were clearly delineated in the personal statement. There is something in almost all of these essays that distinguishes the applicant and stands out in the reader's mind afterward. The applicants reveal themselves as thoughtful and articulate.

(In presenting these examples of successful essays, it is not our intention that you copy from this material in your own application.)

It is, I think, primarily a story of survival, of struggle and success against all odds. It began on urban mean streets in a poor, black, inner-city area where hope is in short supply. For me, raised in a single-parent home, baseball was the ticket out.

Recruited by a university to play ball, I became the first member of my family to receive the opportunity for a college education. At first, my only goal was to endure, to make it through my four years of varsity baseball. I knew, however, that I wanted much more. I left sports, applied myself to my studies (my grades went from basically C's to B's), and was elected vice president of the student body. These were accomplishments I could never have foreseen for myself just a few years earlier.

My success in these endeavors gave me confidence and encouraged me to entertain dreams that earlier would have been unimaginable. I started thinking about the possibility of one day becoming a lawyer so that I could return to my community and help others like myself. In my senior year I took the LSAT, but my scores were not strong and I decided to defer any effort to enter law school. Instead, I took the skills I acquired in student government—in communication and analytical thinking—and began work as a legislative assistant to a state senator from my home district. In this capacity, I constantly spoke to various community organizations, worked in the state capital, and learned much about the whole governmental process.

This work prompted me to seek a Master's in Public Administration, which I earned with a 3.0 GPA even while working nights for the county probation department. As a counselor working with juveniles, I wrote reports for judges and was exposed further to the law and to court procedure. In school, meantime, I studied legal cases and was regularly called upon to recite and interpret them in front of my class. All of these experiences piqued my determination to become a lawyer, but the time was still not right. I began working at the same school I attended as a child, eventually becoming the assistant principal as well as teaching classes. The longer I worked there, the more I knew I had to attend law school.

Where I grew up, one is confronted with unemployment, unstable family life, crime, poverty and, perhaps most sadly, despair. There is also an acute shortage of affordable legal assistance. As an attorney working in this community, I would be able to help educate these people so that they know more about their rights—as tenants, as employees, and as citizens. Even more significantly, I could be an ally and a role model, someone who could help reduce the prevailing sense of helplessness while at the same time raising the level of hope. I could make a difference.

I am well aware of the demands and long hours law school imposes. I know, too, though, that I have the will, intelligence, and stamina to succeed. I have already demonstrated my ability to endure; I have overcome many obstacles and I have survived. I hope you will share my confidence that I will prosper in law school as well. So much depends on your favorable action upon my application.

In 1977 I was accepted into an M.B.A. program in my native New Zealand. However, I decided to postpone my graduate business education until a later date.

In the intervening years I have used my law degree and background in accounting to fill a variety of management positions with a company with annual revenues exceeding $100 million.

Working for various subsidiaries of this firm, I have been involved in reorganizing financial systems, developing and implementing new management reporting systems, negotiating union contracts, and selecting and installing computer systems, as well as, more recently, straight management trouble-shooting.

My work has been challenging, varied, and educational, and in my work environment, I have been granted—and become accustomed to—a high degree of autonomy. I have grown both personally and professionally. I have also learned a good deal about myself as I have functioned in so many diverse situations. I have seen that I am self-confident, aggressive, and ambitious. I have successfully navigated the uncharted waters of a number of unstructured situations by relying on what proved to be strong analytical skills and organizational abilities.

Accomplishing many different kinds of tasks over the past eight years has led me to believe that I can do much more—in fact, achieve whatever goals I set—if only I persevere and continue constantly to learn and to grow.

Others probably perceive me as a directed, capable, energetic, and athletic person. (I have competed, with considerable success, in numerous tennis and swimming contests.) They may also perceive me as someone who at times can be impatient. I have worked successfully with a wide range of individuals, but I hope that as I mature and learn I will become more of a leader.

What is most distinctive about me is that I have an international background, not only as a New Zealander but also as one who has worked extensively in Australia, Canada, Hawaii, and the continental United States. Furthermore, relying on my training as a lawyer, I have been deeply involved in litigation management. For the past three years I have managed a number of high-rise building contract disputes involving protracted negotiations and the drafting of multiparty settlement agreements. As a result, I perhaps have a broader perspective than many others in terms of evaluating business decisions for their legal as well as economic ramifications.

I first became interested in medicine when I entered college in 1978. When it came time to choose my major, I selected psychobiology and, accordingly, studied a curriculum with a strong emphasis on science and psychology.

Then, early in 1981, my mother became terminally ill with cancer. Although there are 5 other children in the family, the responsibility for caring for my mother fell to me. She needed constant care and it was up to me to provide it.

I had to withdraw from one of my classes at school, while commuting to campus for tests in the remaining two classes (my routine with my mother made it impossible for me to attend lectures, so I had to rely heavily on my textbooks and self-study). Despite the trauma I was going through at home, I somehow managed to do well in these two classes (calculus and physics), keeping up at least part of my college career.

For four months, I spoon-fed my mother daily and helped keep her alive. I kept the entire family going, even after my mother's death, when I was emotionally and physically depleted (I had lost 15 pounds during her illness).

After it was all over and I was back on my feet, I decided I wanted to put myself back in a situation in which I could help others who were ill. I started working in the ____ hospital. . . . I also started working as a Student Health Advocate in college, following a ten-week training period, which covered diagnosis, role-playing (responding to "patients" with a wide variety of problems), first aid, and emotional concerns—all followed by extensive testing.

Caring for my mother, working at the hospital, and serving as a Student Health Advocate—all of these experiences have not only solidified my interest in medicine but also have taught me how essential it is that physicians be sensitive to the emotional as well as physical needs of their patients. My life to date has taught me lessons that can't be learned in a classroom, lessons that—with the further academic training I hope to receive in medical school—should make me one exceptional doctor.

At the age of 23 I am fortunate to hold the most significant judicial role available to any student in the 25,000-member academic community. In my position, to which I was elected last spring, I enjoy the opportunity of having constant hands-on experience with the same judicial process within which every attorney works. I have studied penal law and the municipal code, researched cases, met with the parties involved in various disputes, and presided over fourteen trials involving complaints that have evolved into formal charges. . . .

I serve as chairman of committees dealing with concerns as varied as community relations and the revision of the school's judicial constitution.

I began my college career on something less than a fully auspicious note. I naively chose a major not suited to my interests and wound up with my poorest grades ever. However, even as a freshman, I was showing my stripes as a leader, serving as captain of the varsity soccer team and president of my dormitory.

Since my sophomore year, there has been a significant and steady upward trend to my grades, and I have achieved about a 3.7 GPA to date. . . .

I originally became interested in the law during my sophomore year when I realized that my skills as a writer, speaker, and leader—as well as my powers of logic—would probably serve me well in a legal career.

All that I have done and experienced in my judicial role in college has further stimulated and reinforced my interest in the law and my determination to pursue a legal career. I believe that I have much more of an awareness of the law than the average student and a realistic perspective on what the lawyer's life entails.

I grew up in circumstances that provide a classic example of the frequent disparity between appearance and reality. To any outsider, my family might have seemed to be enjoying the ideal upper-middle-class existence: peaceful, pretty, and privileged. In actuality, however, alcohol and domestic violence were creating an environment within our house that, for me, was both difficult and frightening.

My mother had a drinking problem, and the encounters between my father and her often escalated into violence. I spent a great deal of time trying to care for my mother, a fact of my young life that I think later on may have subliminally drawn me toward a career in medicine. Besides instilling within me a desire to help others who are ill, my experience with my mother also heightened my sensitivity to other people and the difficulties with which they sometimes must cope.

I felt some of the same sympathy while working last year with a local doctor in rural Mexico. The poverty and ignorance there, which had much to do with the parasitosis, diarrhea, and other medical problems that we saw, was very affecting. I was impressed by the difference the doctor made in these people's lives and by the appreciation that they demonstrated. I was also fascinated by my venture into an urban Mexican hospital, where I had a chance to observe Caesarean sections, treat a gunshot wound, and assist in the delivery of a child.

Complementing my Mexican experience was my three-month summer internship with an oncologist at a stateside hospital. In this position I had the opportunity to observe many physicians and a variety of surgeries, as well as doctor/patient interactions. I was also exposed to cardiology, orthopedics, and urology—among other specialties—and gained a greater awareness of the compassion and understanding that a good physician must bring to his or her work.

The experiences both here and in Mexico were inspiring to me, and I came away from them with the feeling that I could do similar work and derive great satisfaction from it.

In my personal life, I find pleasure in many different endeavors. I enjoy traveling and have visited Europe, Hong Kong, Indonesia, Tahiti, Cuba, and South America. I also enjoy expressing myself through music. Although I am not a virtuoso on any instrument, I have played the violin since the sixth grade and currently write songs on the piano and guitar. My greatest love, however, is sports, and I participate in everything from competitive tennis and volleyball to cycling and scuba diving.

I know that medical school will require that I summon all of my resources, but I have the commitment and stamina to look forward to it all. It will provide me with the best opportunity to become a productive member of society, while making use of my intellectual talents in a career that I expect to be constantly challenging and fulfilling.

*T*his business school applicant was responding to a question about important accomplishments and the role that personal commitment played.

For the first twenty years of my life, my activities—and self-confidence—were circumscribed by the fact that I was a chronic allergic asthmatic. I was underweight, not as strong or as well as my peers, and unable to participate normally in sports. At night I was unable to sleep without an inhaler beside my bed. I was forced to ingest heavy medication on a daily basis.

At the age of 20 I started running (slowly at first), because I discovered that this exercise—although routinely precipitating a mild asthma attack—would later enable me to sleep through the night.

Very gradually my runs became longer. My strength improved, the severity and frequency of my attacks lessened, and soon I was able to discontinue all medication. More remarkably, after about seven years, I was actually able to run 20 miles with no problem at all. This accomplishment was an enormous confidence booster as it demonstrated that a normal, healthy life was possible for me and that I could achieve anything if I set my mind to it.

Eventually it was a logical step for me to progress into competition. I found myself running in marathons and, finally, competing in triathlons. In 1983, in fact, I successfully competed in the Hawaii Ironman triathlon, arguably the most arduous and certainly the most celebrated single-day athletic endurance event.

I have assiduously pursued aerobic exercise for the past eleven years, ever since I discovered that such endeavors were finally possible for me and were the means by which I could attain physical strength and well-being. It was a long and arduous road for me—from huffing and puffing (and wheezing) my way through tentative 1-mile runs to involving myself in the rigors of the triathlon—but I was determined to become fit and to stay fit.

It has made all the difference.

A s a doctor's son I have been exposed to medicine all my life and independently developed a special interest in the sciences at an early age. It wasn't until my junior year in high school, however, when I saw my father bring a new child into the world, that I knew for sure that I wanted to become a doctor myself.

As I watched my father interacting with the expectant mother, trying to help her relax, then delivering her infant, I was profoundly moved: the expression "the miracle of life" assumed new meaning for me. I realized at that moment that doctors are involved in both the worst and the most wonderful moments in the lives of others and are in a unique position to help out on either type of occasion. . . .

I believe that my summer work in various medical facilities demonstrates my strong interest in and dedication to becoming a doctor, and I feel my grades indicate my aptitude in dealing with the kinds of courses that are a part of every medical school's curriculum. . . .

In 1961, three years before I was born in San Diego, my parents fled their native Cuba to escape communism and the repression of Fidel Castro's regime. They spoke barely a word of English and started their new life in America with little more than the clothes on their backs.

There were no provisions in the 1960s in area schools for Spanish-speaking children, so my early years in the educational system were difficult.

Eventually, though, my academic progress enabled me to take the California Proficiency Exam and score sufficiently well that I was able to skip my senior year of high school and proceed instead to my first year of college.

Now I have become one of the state's youngest real estate brokers and, working 30–40 hours a week for the past two years, I have successfully built a trust fund large enough to subsidize my law school education and to allow me to spend all of my time during those three years concentrating on my studies. Up to now, my efforts in business have detracted from my performance in college; in law school, however, I am confident my grades will more accurately reflect my abilities.

During my childhood my parents were, understandably, unable to respond with much enthusiasm to my often-stated ambition of one day becoming an attorney. They were naturally more concerned with day-to-day survival than anything else and could scarcely dream of ever sending me to college, much less law school.

Just having reached the juncture in my life at which it is possible for me to apply to law school represents the fulfillment of one of my longest-held dreams. It is hard for me to forget my earliest days in school, when I could not even understand most of what my teachers were saying.

It is not surprising, I suppose, that I have a particular interest in the problems of the

Hispanic community. Whatever I could do as a lawyer to help these people who are so victimized by unscrupulous businessmen, as well as their own ignorance of the law, would give me great satisfaction. . . .

W hile my two years of experience in the business world have taught me substantive lessons, I approach my graduate business education with an enthusiasm, flexibility, open-mindedness, and desire to learn that I believe will serve me equally well. After securing an undergraduate degree in business, I have now had the opportunity to see how things actually work in a professional environment. I have developed a passion for business that exceeds anything I expected, as well as the conviction that—with further education and training—I have the potential to attain whatever goals I establish for myself.

I have chosen a field—finance—in which I know I can excel, principally as a result of my strong analytical abilities. One of my significant past achievements drew on just such skills. As an assignment for the real estate company for which I serve as financial analyst, I was to do a cash flow analysis for a $30-million office building that we were set to acquire. My projections for the first-year cash flow turned out—quite amazingly—to be within $10,000 of the actual figures.

The same energy and capabilities which led to my being selected as one of the top 10 (out of more than 500) business students at my undergraduate institution has made me successful in my work endeavors to date, but there is so much more I need to learn. I think the fact that I am a quick study, that I tend to assimilate new material with relative ease and speed, will help me to meet the rigorous academic challenges that your curriculum will pose. I am a detail-oriented person, but I manage to maintain a broad perspective, and I think this will be useful to me in studying for my M.B.A.

I am particularly interested in finance as a cornerstone in the foundation for my career in business. I want to know much more about such things as computer sciences as applied to finance (in terms of projecting financial models) and organizational behavior as it relates to working in groups.

Management consulting is my main professional goal at this point, as I like the idea of a business activity that involves extensive people contact, variety, and working regularly in different settings.

There are several reasons I am confident that I am well suited to a career in business. I am just as comfortable working with people as with numbers and greatly enjoy the personal interaction that is a part of business. I am a well-rounded individual and I regard myself as something of a diplomat, having gracefully dealt with a number of delicate situations in my business experience. I am ambitious, motivated, persistent, and organized and have the capacity for quantitative thinking that business today demands.

When I am not working, I derive pleasure from such diverse activities as reading, traveling, and skiing. Because I also enjoy art and music, I know that I would greatly relish living in the cultural mecca that is *(school's city).*

In 1979, in the Soviet city of Odessa on the Black Sea, a young man confronted a problem that would forever alter the course of his existence. This 17-year-old Jewish man, who wanted most to become a doctor, was denied the possibility of admission to medical school because of his religion. It could have been an end to a dream.

I was that man. My determination to become a physician, and my parents' support of that ambition, turned our lives upside down. We applied for a visa to leave Russia; while we waited, my parents and older brother were not allowed to work, and all of us were followed by the KGB. When we finally arrived in America in 1980, we had to make our way to Seattle without funds, friends, or command of English. My father, who is an engineer, was reduced to working as a plumber, while I began each day at 5 a.m. unloading trucks. Life was a struggle but we were all sustained by a dream: my goal of studying to become a doctor.

Within a year of my arrival here, after attending night school to learn the language, I was able to obtain a job as an X-ray orderly at a local hospital. In this position, and later as an admitting aide, I was able over a period of three years to learn much more about American medicine. I had extensive contact with patients, doctors, nurses, and administrators and found I was able to relate well to each group. I saw suffering, healing, death, and all of the other constants that make up any hospital environment. I had an opportunity to observe surgeries, from mastectomies to hysterectomies and bypasses, and to see firsthand the importance of positive doctor-patient interactions. I was fascinated by everything I saw and became more convinced than ever that I could one day make my finest contribution as a physician.

When I first entered college, I had enormous problems with English, especially scientific terminology, and my GPA was an unremarkable 2.84. However, as I mastered the language, my grades steadily improved; in fact, in the last three quarters, I've earned a 3.8 GPA.

Beginning in 1984, I worked as a volunteer in the autopsy room at my university's pathology department, amassing more than 500 hours' experience. Just as the hospital provided me with a chance to observe diagnosis and treatment, the autopsy room gave me a chance to find out what goes wrong, what causes death. In that room it was possible for me to see death, smell it, touch it. I prepared organs for examination by medical students, as well as assisted in autopsies and cleaning up. I was even awarded a highly sought after scholarship in recognition of my work. . . .

I first became interested in medicine in high school, when I sat in on my brother's medical school lectures and later accompanied him on hospital rounds. My commitment to becoming a doctor, and my excitement over the prospect of being able to serve others in this capacity, is what has driven me and kept me going in the face of so many obstacles since my departure from Russia. Now, with my goal in sight and so many recent experiences reaffirming my passion for medicine, I know that all of the dedication and sacrifice have been worthwhile. I am eager to begin my medical studies, eager to meet the challenges I know they will present.

My decision to return to school now and earn my M.B.A. degree stems from my determination that I have specific needs that can best be met within the confines of a graduate business curriculum. I need more specific general management skills, a greater degree of expertise in data processing and computers, and a broader knowledge of finance (as opposed to accounting) in order to progress in my career.

Being in the business world and residing in your city, I am, of course, well aware of your reputation as one of the premier graduate business schools in the United States. The high caliber of the faculty and student population would provide me with a challenging and highly stimulating environment in which to study. The interplay of ideas would be illuminating and provocative, and the contacts I would establish within the school (and without) could only be assets to me as I continue my career.

The timing of my application to your program seems especially propitious as I will soon be leaving my firm (of my own volition) after eight productive years that have been extremely beneficial to me. I have reached the point at which there are no significant new opportunities available to me in the company that I would find exciting or rewarding. It is time to move on and the perfect moment for me to seek to broaden the business foundation upon which the balance of my career will rest. I am eager to round out my education and fill any gaps that exist in my knowledge and understanding of business theory and the skills necessary to survive and prosper in today's fast-paced, always-changing, high-tech business world.

My interest in science dates back to my years in high school, where I excelled in physics, chemistry, and math. When I was a senior, I took a first-year calculus course at a local college (such an advanced-level class was not available in high school) and earned an A. It seemed only logical that I pursue a career in electrical engineering.

When I began my undergraduate career, I had the opportunity to be exposed to the full range of engineering courses, all of which tended to reinforce and solidify my intense interest in engineering. I've also had the opportunity to study a number of subjects in the humanities and they have been both enjoyable and enlightening, providing me with a new and different perspective on the world in which we live.

In the realm of engineering, I have developed a special interest in the field of laser technology and have even been taking a graduate course in quantum electronics. Among the 25 or so students in the course, I am the sole undergraduate. Another particular interest of mine is electromagnetics, and last summer, when I was a technical assistant at a world-famous local lab, I learned about its many practical applications, especially in relation to microstrip and antenna design. Management at this lab was sufficiently impressed with my work to ask that I return when I graduate. Of course, my plans following completion of my current studies are to move directly into graduate work toward my master's in science. After I earn my master's degree, I intend to start work on my Ph.D. in electrical engineering. Later I would like to work in the area of research and development for private industry. It is in R & D that I believe I can make the greatest contribution, utilizing my theoretical background and creativity as a scientist.

I am highly aware of the superb reputation of your school, and my conversations with several of your alumni have served to deepen my interest in attending. I know that, in addition to your excellent faculty, your computer facilities are among the best in the state. I hope you will give me the privilege of continuing my studies at your fine institution.

Having majored in literary studies (world literature) as an undergraduate, I would now like to concentrate on English and American literature.

I am especially interested in nineteenth-century literature, women's literature, Anglo-Saxon poetry, and folklore and folk literature. My personal literary projects have involved some combination of these subjects. For the oral section of my comprehensive exams, I specialized in nineteenth-century novels by and about women. The relationship between "high" and folk literature became the subject for my honors essay, which examined Toni Morrison's use of classical, biblical, African, and Afro-American folk tradition in her novel. I plan to work further on this essay, treating Morrison's other novels and perhaps preparing a paper suitable for publication.

In my studies toward a doctoral degree, I hope to examine more closely the relationship between high and folk literature. My junior year and private studies of Anglo-Saxon language and literature have caused me to consider the question of where the divisions between folklore, folk literature, and high literature lie. Should I attend your school, I would like to resume my studies of Anglo-Saxon poetry, with special attention to its folk elements.

Writing poetry also figures prominently in my academic and professional goals. I have just begun submitting to the smaller journals with some success and am gradually building a working manuscript for a collection. The dominant theme of this collection relies on poems that draw from classical, biblical, and folk traditions, as well as everyday experience, in order to celebrate the process of giving and taking life, whether literal or figurative. My poetry both draws from and influences my academic studies. Much of what I read and study finds a place in my creative work as subject. At the same time, I study the art of literature by taking part in the creative process, experimenting with the tools used by other authors in the past.

In terms of a career, I see myself teaching literature, writing criticism, and going into editing or publishing poetry. Doctoral studies would be valuable to me in several ways. First, your teaching assistantship program would provide me with the practical teaching experience I am eager to acquire. Further, earning a Ph.D. in English and American literature would advance my other two career goals by adding to my skills, both critical and creative, in working with language. Ultimately, however, I see the Ph.D. as an end in itself, as well as a professional stepping-stone; I enjoy studying literature for its own sake and would like to continue my studies on the level demanded by the Ph.D. program.

I have been planning a career in geological sciences for several years but, as an undergraduate, I concentrated on getting a solid background in math and science. After graduation, I took a job to allow myself time to thoroughly think through my plans and to expose myself to a variety of work situations. This strategy has been very valuable to me in rounding out my career plans.

During the past eighteen months I have had first-hand experience with computers in a wide array of business applications. This has stimulated me to think about ways in which computers could be used for scientific research. One idea that particularly fascinates me is mathematical modeling of natural systems, and I think those kinds of techniques could be put to good use in geological science. I have always enjoyed and been strong in areas that require logical, analytical thought, and I am anxious to combine my interest in earth science with my knowledge of, and aptitude for, computer-related work. There are several specific areas that I have already studied that I think would lend themselves to research based on computing techniques, including mineral phase relations in igneous petrology and several topics in structural geology.

I have had both lecture/lab and field courses in structural geology, as well as a short module dealing with plate tectonics, and I am very interested in the whole area. I would like to explore structural geology and tectonics further at the graduate level. I am also interested in learning more about geophysics. I plan to focus on all these areas in graduate school, while at the same time continuing to build up my overall knowledge of geology.

My ultimate academic goal is to earn a Ph.D., but enrolling first in a master's program will enable me to explore my various interests and make a more informed decision about which specific discipline I will want to study in depth.

As far as long-term plans, I hope to get a position at a university or other institution where I can indulge my primary impulse, which is to be involved in scientific research, and also try my hand at teaching.

My longtime fascination with politics and international affairs is reflected in my participation, starting in high school, in activities such as student council, school board meetings, Vietnam war protests, the McCarthy campaign, and the grape boycott. As each new cause came along, I was always ready to go to Washington or the state capital to wave a sign or chant slogans. Although I look back on these activities today with some chagrin, I realize they did help me to develop, at an early age, a sense of concern for social and political issues and a genuine desire to play a role.

As an undergraduate, I was more interested in social than academic development. During my last two years, I became involved with drugs and alcohol and devoted little time to my studies, doing only as much as was necessary to maintain a B average. After graduation my drug use became progressively worse; without the motivation or ability to look for a career job, I worked for a time in a factory and then, for three years, as a cab driver in New York City.

In 1980 I finally "hit bottom" and became willing to accept help. I joined both Alcoholics Anonymous and Narcotics Anonymous and for the next several years the primary business of my life was recovery. Although I had several "slips" in the beginning, I have now enjoyed nearly seven years of complete freedom from drug and alcohol use. I mention my bout with addiction because I think it is important in answering two issues that presumably will be of concern to the admissions committee: my lackluster undergraduate record and the fact that I have waited until the age of 34 to begin preparing academically for a career in public policy. It would be an oversimplification to call addiction the cause for either of these things; rather I would say it was the most obvious manifestation of an underlying immaturity that characterized my postadolescent years. More importantly, the discipline of recovery has had a significant impact on my overall emotional growth.

During the last years of my addiction I was completely oblivious to the world around me. Until 1983 I didn't even realize that there had been a revolution in Nicaragua or that one was going on in El Salvador. Then I rejoined the Quaker Meeting, in which I had been raised as a child, and quickly gravitated to its Peace and Social Order Committee. They were just then initiating a project to help refugees from Central America and I joined enthusiastically in the work. I began reading about Central America and, later, teaching myself Spanish. I got to know refugees who were victims of poverty and oppression, became more grateful for my own economic and educational advantages, and developed a strong desire to give something back by working to provide opportunities to those who have not been so lucky.

In 1986 I went to Nicaragua to pick coffee for two weeks. This trip changed my whole outlook on both the United States and the underdeveloped world. The combination of living for two weeks amid poverty and engaging in long political discussions with my fellow coffee pickers, including several well-educated professionals who held views significantly to the left of mine, profoundly shook my world view. I came back humbled, aware of how little I knew about the world and eager to learn more. I began raiding the public library for everything I could find on the Third World and started subscribing to a wide variety of periodicals, from scholarly journals such as *Foreign Affairs* and *Asian Survey,* to obscure newsletters such as *Through Our Eyes* (published by U.S. citizens living in Nicaragua).

Over the intervening two years, my interest has gradually focused on economics. I have come to realize that economic development (including equitable distribution of wealth) is the key to peace and social justice, both at home and in the Third World. I didn't study economics in college and have found it difficult to understand the economic issues that are at the heart of many policy decisions. At the same time, though, I am fascinated by the subject. Given my belief that basic economic needs are among the most fundamental of human rights, how can society best go about providing for them? Although I call myself an idealist, I'm convinced that true idealism must be pragmatic. I am not impressed, for example, by simplistic formulations that require people to be better than they are. As a Quaker I believe that the means are inseparable from the end; as an American I believe that democracy and freedom of expression are essential elements of a just society, though I'm not wedded to the idea that our version of democracy is the only legitimate one.

Although I have carved out a comfortable niche in my present job, with a responsible position and a good salary, I have become increasingly dissatisfied with the prospect of a career in business applications programming. More and more of my time and energy is now being absorbed by community activities. After getting my master's in public administration, I would like to work in the area of economic development in the Third World, particularly Latin America. The setting might be a private (possibly church-based) development agency, the UN, the OAS, one of the multilateral development banks, or a government agency. What I need from graduate school is the academic foundation for such a career. What I offer in return is a perspective that comes from significant involvement in policy issues at the grass roots level, where they originate and ultimately must be resolved.

THE
INSIDE
PERSPECTIVE

Advice from Admissions Representatives of Leading Professional and Graduate Schools

The Business Schools

John E. Flowers
Director of Admissions and Financial Aid
The Wharton School (University of Pennsylvania)

We're looking for clarity, power, and force, especially in terms of articulating why one wants the M.B.A. and how one is going to use it. We expect people to weave into the argument for the necessity of doing the M.B.A. past experience and past education, which provides a kind of springboard or foundation in the business school for a career beyond. We expect that there be a fair degree of focus about what one wants to do and a very clear articulation of that. I don't mean a narrow and myopic view. We don't expect people to say, "I want *x* kind of job in *x* company," but we do need fairly well defined, clear parameters within which the individual sees his or her career developing. So the basic idea is to present a kind of argument in which the past is united with the future, and the M.B.A. plays the part of the string or glue which holds the package together.

Applicants make a mistake in not knowing what they want to do and not being very clear about their rationale for getting the M.B.A. Another mistake is not completely articulating what opportunities they've exploited in the past and what opportunities they're looking for in the future. Then there are all the usual kinds of things like sloppiness, typos, bad grammar, and general lack of care. We sometimes say to ourselves as we evaluate applications, "Would this individual submit this kind of work in a business report or a business plan?" We expect people to take the same kind of care with presentation (as well as content) as they would in the management setting.

There are 5 people on the admissions committee, but only one person sees all of the applications. Each application is seen by at least 2 people and sometimes as many as 5.

Lee Cunningham
Director of Admissions and Aid
The University of Chicago Graduate School of Business

We're looking for people who have some notion of the direction they want their academic stay here to take and how that relates to their professional goals. So we're looking for people who have at least some rudimentary sense of direction as far as both the program here and professional goals are concerned.

The mistake people make most often is not to look at what the questions are asking. Some people prepare generic statements because they're applying to more than one school and it's a lot of work to do a personal essay for each school. On the other hand, it detracts when we realize that we're one of six schools and the applicant is saying the same thing to each and every school, despite the fact that there are actually critical differences between the kinds of schools they may be applying to. They don't take the time. They underestimate the kind of attention that's paid to these essays. Take a look at what the essay asks and deal with those issues articulately and honestly.

At least 2, and sometimes 3, people read each essay. I read them to make the final decision. Our process works so that each person who reads the application does a written evaluation of what he or she has read—and the written evaluations are not seen by the other reader.

Richard A. Silverman
Director of Admissions and External Relations
Yale School of Organization and Management

There's no single type of essay we're looking for; there's no "correct" response to the essay questions that we pose. What are we looking for? First, we're looking for information to fill in the blanks in a person's résumé. We want to know what our applicants have done and what they want to do in the future, what their values are, and how they relate their values to their work. We're also interested in how they write. The form of the essays can be important, as well as the content. How applicants handle the English language is important—the ability to articulate their thoughts in a clear and concise way. In a school with a surplus of qualified candidates, decisions are made for reasons that can't be reduced to numbers or facts in some formulaic way. Essays help our Admissions Committee do what it must do, which is to reach reasoned, yet ultimately subjective, judgments. You will find if you inquire from school to school that the importance of the essays increases as the selectivity of the admissions process increases.

In one essay we ask students, in effect, to rationalize their past and connect it to their future. We call this the "career objectives" essay. It gives us hard information, but it is also a way of determining if applicants are capable of thinking reflectively—and synthetically— about themselves and their careers. Often, even the most intelligent, by traditional measures, are not.

Our second essay is about learning goals and is designed to provide information about the applicant's reasons for wanting to attend the Yale School of Management in particular. What does he or she expect to learn, and how will this learning be put to use?

One common "mistake" in essays is to narrate one's résumé, or life history, without any reflection or evaluation or self-criticism. Another mistake is to write "what the Admissions Office wants to hear," which usually turns out to be very artificial sounding at best. There is also the person who is low key to the point of not telling us very much. We call this the "British understatement problem." It's not always a mistake; in fact, it often makes for a refreshing change after countless self-glorifying essays (another pitfall). But in some cases an applicant simply doesn't say much, and we can't tell if it's because of modesty, lack of expressive ability, or possibly because he or she hasn't given much thought to what we're trying to do with the essays or with application information generally.

Advice? Don't send first drafts. Write essays and then sit on them for a while. Try to be as clear and concise as possible, but don't let the school's length limitations prevent you from being thorough. Between thoroughness and terseness, there is a happy medium, however; and most essays are too long—or rather, more are too long than too short.

The best approach is simply to answer the school's questions as thoughtfully and honestly as you can. Let the admissions people make the admissions decisions. Don't try to psych out the process and make the decision for them. Don't try to pretend to be the stereotype that you think the school has in mind because, when you do that, you probably won't convey much of your own personality or your own thoughts.

Again, be honest. Honesty and openness are virtues in essay writing, as in work and life, as is (maybe) a little risk-taking. People often think that the only applicants who succeed in management school admissions are those who have very precise ideas of what they want to do with the next forty years of their lives. You, in fact, might be rather indecisive at this stage of your life. You might be coming to a period of reexamination. You feel like re-tooling, turning a page, changing direction; but you don't yet know exactly which way you want to go. If that's the case, say it. We've been around a long time and we understand quite well that some of our best students, and many future managerial leaders, go through this kind of "passage." It is much better to be honestly undecided about your future than falsely precise. On the other hand, vagueness is not a virtue, and it would be misleading not to say that most good applicants display in their essays a strong sense of purpose.

Margaret Tyler
Director of Master's Admissions
Sloan School of Management (MIT)

The Statement of Objectives must be well written. You need to be able to effectively communicate your reasons for wanting to do graduate work in management and your sense of commitment. This is not an easy thing to do on paper. Clarity of purpose is important: what do you want to get out of the program, what skills do you hope to develop in the process, and how do you envision using your education in the future?

We require only one statement, but many of our applicants make the mistake of wasting precious space reiterating information contained in other parts of the application. You should use well your opportunity by clarifying and/or expanding on areas that are not automatically obvious either through a résumé or through the other questions asked on the application.

You should not make too many assumptions. Do not assume that the reader has a clear sense of your professional and educational background because you work for a certain organization or because you attended a certain school. This is particularly important for international candidates from environments that are very different from ours.

Finally, this is no time to be unduly modest. You need to articulate your strengths and explain whatever may be perceived as a weakness in your application.

We have a rather interesting process. The statement is read first by an admissions officer, myself or 1 of my 2 colleagues. We read the entire application, writing an assessment that is usually a paragraph long and that makes a recommendation concerning admission. Then it goes to a faculty member who works in the area in which the student has expressed an interest, such as finance or corporate strategy. This faculty person will read the application, write an assessment, and make some commentary on whether or not the student should be admitted. The applicant is then reviewed by the admissions committee, which compares the student to the rest of the pool. At that point the admissions committee will make a decision.

Steven DeKrey
Director of Admissions and Financial Aid
J. L. Kellogg Graduate School of Management (Northwestern University)

We're looking for a well-written, detailed essay that responds directly to the question. The questions are about extracurriculars, motivation, challenges, commitment to the school—that kind of thing. We see a variety and that's fine. Our approach is very individualized. The way the applicant devises the answer—determines the length, develops the response—is all part of the answer. The level of effort applicants put into essays varies considerably, which sends messages to the admissions committee as well. Over-involved, elaborate essays send one message, while very brief and superficial essays send another message.

Trying to second-guess what we are looking for is a common mistake—which we can sense.

We can tell when applicants try to use answers to other schools' questions for our essays; we're sensitive to this. Poorly written essays are a bad reflection on the applicant.

Don't over-elaborate; we're reading a lot of these. Also, don't be too brief or superficial. We like to have major ideas presented well.

Muhammad Abdullah
Senior Associate Director of Admissions
UCLA Graduate School of Management

UCLA is interested in admitting people, not credentials, and the essays are where you meet the people. The personal statement is important in terms of putting in context other parts of the application, and it is important in the fine-tuning stage, particularly in sorting out among qualified applicants those who are the most appealing, the most deserving, and the best matched with us. The essays also give us a look at the value-added effect: the value of the M.B.A. degree for that student as well as how much that student would enrich those who are already here.

People will sometimes comment on our approach, which might be different from some of the other top-tiered schools. To the extent that people let us know that they are aware of that, it certainly shows they've done their homework, that they know what kind of institution we are.

A primary mistake is not to take the essays seriously enough. We take them seriously, so the applicants should, too. They need to take the time to do a good job, and they need to be sure to answer the questions we raise.

I think it's important for applicants to be themselves. I want to get to know the applicant and he or she has to give us a chance to do that. My advice is: Write an essay that reflects you; try to be what you are and let your personality come through.

Applicants should give a frank assessment of their own abilities and put into context things that might be perceived as weaknesses. Of course, there's a thin line between doing this and making excuses. Some students become interested in learning later than others so maybe their first year or two of undergraduate performance was not particularly stellar. The last couple of years might provide a more indicative performance because they've gotten serious. That's helpful and that's something that might come from the essay more clearly than from any-place else.

Enhance those things that make you unique and special.

A prospective student gains something from doing the essays because it helps him or her to crystallize this thinking.

The statements are always seen by at least 2 or 3 people. Besides the admissions people, we also call upon faculty and top-level administra-tors when we think we have cases for which their input would be very valuable. We also have readers among our students who are going to be graduating.

Marda E. Collett
Former Assistant Director of Admissions
The Amos Tuck School (Dartmouth College)

We're looking for someone who can write clearly and concisely. We like to see there has been some thought put into the whole process, that the application hasn't been spieled off in an afternoon or a Sunday evening. We're trying to get a little bit better feel for the individual; we're concerned about how the individual will contribute to the student body and how Tuck will benefit him or her. A "fit" is important.

We're looking for some evidence as to why the applicants want the M.B.A., the motivation behind it, and why it is important at this particular point in their lives. We also look for goal orientation—where they're headed. Sometimes they can be specific, sometimes they can't, but we want to be sure that the individuals have thought through the commitment involved.

Mistakes? The application itself is often the first and only impression. In terms of just the actual technicalities, they don't proofread, they are sloppy, they are not professional. We're looking for a professional presentation in the application itself. Applicants should proofread, be neat, and spell correctly.

Be specific and answer the question directly, without a lot of extras. We prefer applicants to be sensitive to the word limitation that we've set. We have a lot of applications to read and it can be somewhat of an annoyance to have to read six pages when we've asked for two or three.

Applicants should always avoid writing what they think the admissions committee wants to hear. Their writing should let their personality come through while still being professional and serious. Oftentimes we'll read an application and at the end we'll say, "But I don't get a sense of the person here. He or she said all the right things, but it's a generic essay; it could have been used for any institution. Why Tuck, why now, what is it about the applicant's feelings and background that make him or her different from the others?" He or she should get that across to us through that personal statement.

At least 3 people read the essay and it could be as many as 6 or 8.

Judith Goodman
Director of Admissions and Student Services
University of Michigan School of Business Administration

We're looking for a clear, concise response. We're also looking for appropriate or correct English, good writing skills, and some indication of focus in career objective. We do not want to bring in someone who doesn't know yet what he or she wants to do. If the applicant is not sure if the next step should be the M.B.A. degree, then that needs to be given careful consideration before he or she becomes a really viable candidate for the program.

Whatever the person wants to say in the essay is up to him or her. We bring *individuals* in, the class is heterogeneous; we're not looking for everyone to fit in the same mold.

Whatever the question is, we want to see that they've thought the answer through and that it makes sense in terms of the way they've stated it. They need to understand what the M.B.A. can do for them and maybe what it cannot do as well.

Typical mistakes are technical or grammatical errors. Some of these we can forgive because some of them are typos. I think sometimes the individual is not as concise as he or she should be; sometimes, however, they're too *short* in their response.

A person should plan to have enough time because it is usually a difficult process. You do need to feel motivated and creative when you sit down to write or at least jot down some ideas. So, if you allow enough time, you can begin your thought process, make an outline, jot down ideas, come back to it, rewrite, and get it into what you think is the final form. It might not be a bad idea to have someone who knows you read the essays to see if they make sense. Then, if something is really askew in the thought process, you can try to clarify it. And critique it yourself for good grammar and structure.

If there is quick agreement, only 2 to 3 people will read each essay. If there is disagreement, then the entire committee would get involved, which means a total of 4 or 5.

Joyce E. Cornell
Assistant Dean for Admissions
Columbia Business School

We're looking at the way applicants organize their thoughts and express them in writing. We have five major essays on our application so a very good part of the effort involved is doing the writing. From that we're looking for a sense of the applicants' personalities, their interests, and the way they solve problems. We're also looking for a sense of focus and an understanding of what role this education might play in their goals. We look to see if applicants have answered the questions asked. A surprising number of people don't do that; they answer what they want to answer, which may or may not be what we asked. We ask what we ask for a reason; it's not just to get them to put pen to paper. Sometimes applicants give the questions short shrift. When they do that, they've lost the opportunity to present themselves to us.

Applicants should be themselves. It's very hard to dissemble in an application this comprehensive because all the essays are looked at in conjunction with other corroborative information, which involves documentation of activities and accomplishments, transcripts, and references. To tell us in the application that you've always wanted to be a product manager and then have no evidence that you've ever been acquainted with anything similar, or done anything related to it, would be unconvincing. So you might write an essay that in isolation is coherent, but it won't fit into the whole picture well. That certainly diminishes the whole of the application.

Michael S. Wynne
Assistant Dean for Admissions and Advising
New York University Graduate School of Business Administration

At the risk of belaboring the obvious, what strikes people is the overall appearance of the essays. Do they look like they've been put together neatly and carefully? It's not really of primary importance, but we are dealing with human beings here—in terms of the admissions people—and it's good to make a nice impression on them.

Secondly, what strikes one is the overall written communication skills. How effectively do applicants use the language? Is the way they present things appealing and clear?

A third factor would be content. What are they telling you? Does it make sense? Does it seem appropriate, given the program the person is interested in? Admissions committees really want to be convinced. These programs are very demanding, long, and costly. Applicants have to prove they know what they're doing and have adequate motivation.

People are sloppy; they violate some of the basic rules of grammar and word usage. When you're in a competitive situation, you lose a few points for that because you are, supposedly, presenting yourself as best you can. Another mistake involves being either too short or too long. We mention 300 words; when I get to 300 words, or roughly thirty lines, I draw a line—I don't read any more.

When you're competing with this kind of application pool, you really should do your best to provide a succinct, thorough range of information in the space that you're allowed. Succinct but thorough: that's a tough line to walk. Be truthful. You're going to come off a little phony if the essay is not genuine.

An average of 4 people read the statements. When the decisions are more difficult, the entire committee frequently gets involved and that means as many as 8 people.

The Law Schools

Molly Geraghty
Former Director of Admissions
Harvard Law School

When you're trying to put together a diverse class, by definition there's no one single thing—in terms of content—you're looking for. You want it to be well written and interesting. To some extent, it serves a function of an interview, although it's much better—from the applicant's point of view—because the applicant can control it and be sure to say what needs to be said. One of the things it should be is a piece of modern, persuasive, fluid English prose. We do not ask "Why do you want to be a lawyer?" I think a large number of people haven't the remotest idea of why they want to be a lawyer. They may think they do, but things are going to change over time. People come to us from a variety of disciplines and have a lot of different expectations of the legal profession. So we leave the statement very, very open-ended.

People are too cautious; they seem to be eager to please and so they come out with vapid, harmless little pieces of writing. Also, they tend to be a little bit too general.

They ought to sit down and write it, and then give it a very serious rewrite. Then they should show it to someone they know well and whose judgment they trust. And the question to that friend shouldn't be "Is this a dynamite personal statement?"; the question should be, "Does this sound like me?" In other words, there's a certain sense of a person ringing true, and I think that is of considerable value. And often friends can be a judge of that.

I read every statement and nobody gets in without at least 2 others reading it. I can deny it (the application) so it goes no farther than me.

Professor Thomas C. Heller
Member, Admissions Committee
Stanford Law School

I'm interested in the way the person who is applying chooses to present himself or herself in a short essay. I'm interested in what it is about the whole human being that the person selects as being the most essential features relevant to his or her application to school. So I am generally unimpressed with essays that are lists of things that have been done. I'm relatively impressed, on the opposite side, by someone who's able to determine some feature about his or her background or work that they're content to have stand for their general capacities or their general interests. I'm looking for their mode of representing themselves. I'm looking for someone who has carefully thought through the problem of self-presentation and is going to do it in some way that is not trite and that demonstrates either some ambition or some accomplishment with reasonable specificity.

One woman wrote a beautiful piece about what playing basketball for her university had meant to her, why it was important, and what it meant that she was going to be giving it up at this moment in her life.

I'm impressed with people who are writing about what they have done in the immediate past or what they plan to do in the immediate future. As the essay starts to range widely around the five or six years before and after the date of application, I tend to lose interest in it. A statement that describes some project in which they've engaged in the relatively immediate past probably gives an indication of how that person chooses to allocate their time and activities at this stage of their life.

I don't care whether someone is coming out of biology or English or out of business school, but I don't want someone who is trying to escape from something, someone for whom law school is a discontinuous experience rather than one that is building upon something. Sometimes an essay indicates a person is seeking to go to law school to remedy some sort of dissatisfaction they feel in their life.

Each essay is read by 2 or 3 people.

Frances E. Spurgeon
Dean for Admissions
University of Pennsylvania Law School

I'm not interested in why they want to go to law school. A lot of law schools ask that question but we don't. Many of our students are not going to be practicing attorneys; they want the degree for other reasons (and that's not a negative at all), so I don't want to read 3,400 pieces of paper explaining why they want to go to law school. We use this personal statement to find out about this person and what he or she has been doing because we do not have personal interviews here—and most law schools do not. We want to know what their interests are, what their activities have been. It's not used as a writing sample (although I think a lot of students think it is), but if we hit a very poorly written one, of course, that's a negative. It's more information than anything else. Some are very, very informative and some tell you nothing.

I received a great personal statement from a girl who concentrated strictly on an experience that she had had during the summer in Egypt and Israel. That's all she talked about, but she tied it together with her interest in law and it was just a beautifully developed thing. We accepted a military man whose personal statement was just fascinating; it read like a novel. There is not a place on this earth he has not been.

One mistake is when applicants don't tell us anything about themselves, when that's what we're really trying to find out. Or they talk too much about the fact that they were president of their fraternity.

The personal statement is a very important part of the application because you can get very excited about someone through reading it. Or you can just have the feeling that "nothing is coming through here at all."

I read all of the essays. Then we have a faculty admissions committee that reads another 500 or 600. So we have a minimum of 2 readers and a maximum of 5. We are a very small law school; we can only seat about 225 people in the first-year class (from 3,400 applicants), so we're being very selective.

Michael D. Rappaport
Assistant Dean—Admissions
UCLA School of Law

Applicants should take the time to look at what the law school is asking them to write about. At UCLA, we say, "we know you have lots of extracurricular activities—we want to know how you differ, what makes you unique? What can you bring to the first-year class that's going to make you distinctive from the other 99 people who are already there?" The fact that you were active in your fraternity or sorority is really not going to do it. What we're looking for is somebody who, in their personal statement, stands out as being so unusual, so diverse, that they're extremely attractive as a law student for the first-year class. Maybe what's going to make them distinctive is the fact they spent six months living in a log cabin in Alaska. You try to give the law school some justification for admitting you. With a lot of people, there's nothing that's going to make them distinctive. If that's the case, they've got to recognize that, indeed, the essay is not going to make that much difference here at UCLA.

We're also asking if there's any reason their LSAT or grades are not predictive. You'd be amazed at the number of people who completely ignore this—they don't take advantage of the opportunity.

Most law schools operate fairly similarly. There's a certain group of applicants whose grades and LSAT scores are so high that the presumption is that the applicants are going to be admitted unless they do something terribly stupid to keep themselves out. I have seen applicants whose personal statement has done that, but it's extremely rare. At the other extreme is another group of applicants who—no matter what they write—are not going to get in.

The applicant has to realize, first of all, where he or she stands. If you have a straight-A grade point average and a perfect LSAT score, you don't have to spend a lot of time worrying about your personal statement. On the other hand, if you know you're in the borderline area, that's where the personal statement becomes very, very important.

The applicant should take the time to read the application to see what the schools are asking for. Sometimes the school will ask for a general description of why you want to go to law school, or why they should admit you, something of that nature. In such case you can be fairly sure the school is just interested in the essay to see how well you write. So what you say isn't as important as how you say it. On the other hand, some schools are more specific—UCLA being a very good example of that.

Make sure the essay is grammatically and technically correct and well written. Avoid sloppy essays, coffee-stained essays, or ones that are handwritten so you can't read them. You'd be amazed at what we get!

Beth O'Neil
Director of Admissions and Financial Aid
University of California at Berkeley School of Law (Boalt Hall)

We're trying to gauge the potential for a student's success in law school, and we determine that, principally, on the basis of what the student has done in the past. The personal statement carries the responsibility of presenting the student's life experiences.

Applicants make a mistake by doing a lot of speculation about what they're going to do in the future rather than telling us about what they've done in the past. It is our job to speculate, and we are experienced at that.

Applicants also tend to state and not evaluate. They give a recitation of their experience but no evaluation of what effect that particular experience had on them, no assessment of what certain experiences or honors meant.

They also fail to explain errors or weaknesses in their background. Even though we might wish to admit a student, sometimes we can't in view of a weakness that they haven't made any effort to explain. For example, perhaps they haven't told us that they were ill on the day they took the LSAT or had an automobile accident on the way. Such things are legitimate reasons for poor performance. I mean, we understand that life is tough sometimes. We need to know what happened, for example, to cause a sudden drop in the GPA.

Another mistake is that everyone tries to make himself or herself the perfect law school applicant who, of course, does not exist and is not nearly as interesting as a real human being.

Between 1 and 5 people read each application.

Olivia Birdsall
Senior Admissions Counselor
University of Michigan Law School

Our personal statement is very undirected in the sense that we don't ask for any particular thing to be said, or question to be discussed, or aspect to be covered. We want to have the candidate impress us with what he or she thinks is important. So these things can be extremely varied. I could show you a wonderful personal statement, and it would be very unlikely that anyone else could duplicate it because it's essentially an individual essay. The ones that are really the best are the ones that stand out. The others don't give one a sense of really gaining an insight into the applicant. The essential thing about the personal statement is how one views oneself.

Don't be gimmicky: that generally is off-putting. Don't make it overly long. Be clear. This essay is an opportunity to show an aspect of oneself that cannot be shown by either the LSAT or grades. It's an insight into the intellectual lives of the applicants; we want to know what has influenced them and where they're going.

One admissions officer makes the final decision.

Albert R. Turnbull
Associate Dean for Admissions and Placement
University of Virginia School of Law

Until about four years ago, we used the stimulus, "Give us in 200 words or so your reason for wanting to go to law school." We became dissatisfied because the responses we were getting, particularly from undergraduates, were repetitive, bland, and not very helpful in getting a handle on the individual involved. Eventually, the stimulus became, "Write on a matter of interest to you," the purpose to be quite open-ended. Non-undergraduates still focus on why they're applying to law school at this particular time in their lives, but our new stimulus has produced a much more individualized and helpful addition to the application folder because oftentimes it tends to mesh with and complement the lists of extracurricular activities. We get a very wide range of approaches, from poems to essays on economics. We're looking for style and writing ability to some extent, as well as additional insight about the applicant.

Applicants make a mistake when they try to write something they think will please the committee. When they try to anticipate what that might be, they run a great danger of going astray.

The best statements we get reflect the individual in an honest, genuine, and effective manner and thereby project to us an additional dimension that may be inadequately developed in the rest of the application. A lot of time needs to be put in on the crafting of the essay once the applicant decides on the subject.

Of the 3,500 applications, every one gets at least one careful read by a professional admissions person on the admissions committee. The more complicated cases go on to second and third reviews and maybe more.

Jean Webb
Director of Admissions
Yale Law School

Yale Law School does not require a personal statement. We ask for a 250-word essay on a subject of any interest. If an applicant also wants to submit a personal statement, he or she is welcome to do so. We don't consider the application incomplete without the 250-word essay if the applicant sends something longer or sends a personal statement instead, but that's not what we've asked them to do—and faculty readers have varying opinions on the importance of the essay and the importance of following instructions. The 250-word essays are very short—approximately one double-spaced page—so we look to see how well people can express themselves in a short space. The essay ought to be well written, by which I mean that grammar, spelling, and organization should be right.

The essay ought to be authentic. An applicant ought not to write about something because he or she thinks that's what someone else wants to read. The applicant clearly should choose something in which he or she has an interest and perhaps some passion.

Four people typically read each essay.

The Medical Schools

Dr. Norman D. Anderson
Chairman, Committee on Admissions
The Johns Hopkins University School of Medicine

The personal statement is used in a variety of ways: to gain some insight into the applicant's overall personality and background, as well as commitment and motivation; as a personal profile; and to gauge the ability of the individual to discuss thoughts cohesively and in a very intelligent manner. A few people are looking not only at the use of English structure and expression but also at organization and punctuation.

In the statement, the applicants have a real chance to provide more insights into themselves and their backgrounds than are seen simply on a college transcript or even in letters of recommendation—and often they fail to do this. Other people delve into creative writing—telling short anecdotal stories—and that's often a mistake. The individual who sends us an anatomical diagram of the hand, or limericks, is adding very little to the application. They're almost frivolous and they can be construed as such by the reader. One of the more serious criticisms involves essays that are really egocentric. If these are not substantiated by achievements, these can do somewhat of a disservice to the individual. Some people seem to put these together in a great hurry with no thought. They're disorganized and have no continuity of thought or flow of English expression. Sloppy, poorly punctuated essays seem almost to be a challenge to the reader.

I read all the statements. There will also be appraisals by at least 2 and sometimes as many as 6 faculty members.

Tania Friedman
Admissions Officer
Harvard Medical School

The essay is the one part of the application in which the applicant can present himself or herself other than through somebody else's eyes. Mostly we're looking for a sense of commitment. We also want to see how well the applicant expresses himself or herself. What feeling does the essay give you? Does the applicant come across as a thinking person, a feeling person, someone who seems to be sensitive about issues? Does the applicant have any qualities of leadership or originality? Certainly if someone has a good writing style, that is an advantage, but we're not really grading it as an English essay. We're looking at it in terms of how the person is expressing his or her commitment to medicine.

Write it as simply and straightforwardly as you can. Try not to sound apologetic. If you have some unusual circumstances you want to portray, state them simply. For example, if a student has had to take time off from school because a parent is dying, that's understandable, that's enough of a statement. We understand what has to be going on with a person who's losing a parent. It's a devastating circumstance to be in.

Some people may be brilliant scientists and become very compassionate physicians, but it's not possible for them to discuss themselves in a self-enhancing manner. Some people do it very well and others don't. We have to evaluate the sum of the record.

Usually 2 people read the statements.

Dr. Andrew G. Frantz
Chairman, Committee on Admissions
College of Physicians and Surgeons (Columbia University)

We look for honesty (as far as we can discern it), simplicity, straightforwardness. I tend to be put off by too many self-congratulatory statements, such as, "I'm an excellent candidate for medical school; I have great compassion"—that kind of thing. One person wrote, "As part of my personality, I radiate a high degree of warmth and sincerity"—and that was not good.

Try to sound natural. A lot of students would like to think that maybe they can somehow talk themselves into medical school, especially if their application is otherwise average or mediocre. They think there's some golden combination of words that, if only they can find it, will unlock the doors and get them in. I just don't think that's true.

It shouldn't be too long. Our application forms have a certain amount of space, and we prefer that the candidates don't go over that. Some people seem afflicted with a desire to write novel-length statements and those are difficult to read. Why do most people want to become doctors? They want to help other people, they're interested in science, and medicine seems to represent a good combination of both these impulses. Making the whole statement too lengthy or too flowery doesn't do them any good. Grammatical mistakes are bad. Spelling mistakes I tend to forgive because spelling is not perfectly correlated with intelligence, and even people who are quite bright can make spelling mistakes. But if it's full of spelling mistakes, that's not encouraging.

Our form used to ask, "Why do you want to be a doctor?", but eight or nine years ago we changed it to, "What satisfaction do you expect to receive from being a doctor?" A lot of people don't answer it; they just write their standard essay.

Some students have told me that they plan to spend a good part of their summer working on their essay, and I think that's nonsense. My own feeling is that the essay has been more a cause of people getting downgraded than being favorably judged, usually because it is too contrived or patently insincere. As an admissions committee member, after you've gone through thirty or forty such applications in an afternoon, you're so grateful for somebody who just says something simply and straightforwardly. The poor people who are reading these don't want highly wrought compositions.

Dr. Thomas Lentz
Assistant Dean for Admissions
Yale University School of Medicine

We simply ask for a personal profile, which is pretty open. It allows applicants to say whatever they want to say about themselves, what they would like to bring to the attention of the admissions committee. Most of the time people discuss their reasons for being interested in medicine. Others may discuss particular interests or hobbies or accomplishments. People also use it to explain deficiencies in their application. We view the personal profile as a supplement that the student perhaps can use to enhance his or her application.

People sometimes write an unusual type of essay and they do it intentionally, I'm sure, to draw attention to themselves. For example, they'll tell a story or they'll write a poem. I have mixed feelings about this. Occasionally, some of these will merge into the bizarre category and make you wonder about the stability of the applicant. A few of them, though, are quite good and creative. You've got thousands of applications and 90 percent of the essays sound the same, so some people will try to be different.

Be forthright and honest, and explain sincerely why you want to become a physician. If you can convey some of that desire and motivation through the essay, that might help a little bit.

Two people see the statement initially and then—if the person is to be interviewed—2 more people who will do the interview. In our system, the interviewers will summarize the application to the committee, and occasionally they will call attention to something in the essay if it's particularly good or bad.

Dr. Daniel R. Alonso
Associate Dean for Admissions
Cornell University Medical College

We look for some originality because nine out of ten essays leave you with a big yawn. "I like science, I like to help people and that's why I want to be a doctor." The common, uninteresting, and unoriginal statement is one that recounts the applicant's academic pursuits and basically repeats what is elsewhere in the application. You look for something different, something that will pique your interest and provide some very unique insight that will make you pay some notice to this person who is among so many other qualified applicants. If you're screening 5,500 applications over a four- or six-month period, you want to see something that's really interesting.

I would simply say: Do it yourself, be careful, edit it, go through as many drafts as necessary. And more important than anything: be yourself. Really show your personality. Tell us why you are unique, why we should admit you. The premise is that 9 out of 10 people who apply to medical school are very qualified. Don't under any circumstances insert handwritten work or an unfinished piece of writing. Do a professional job. I would consider it a mistake to attempt to cram in too much information, too many words. Use the space as judiciously as possible. Don't submit additional pages *or* use only 1/20th of the space provided.

Dr. John Herweg
Chairman, Committee on Admissions
Washington University School of Medicine

We are looking for a clear statement that indicates that the applicant can use the English language in a meaningful and effective fashion. We frankly look at spelling as well as typing (for errors both in grammar and composition). Most applicants use the statement to indicate their motivation for medicine, the duration of that motivation, extracurricular activities, and work experience. So those are some of the general things we are looking for in the Personal Comments section.

We also want applicants to personalize the statement, to tell us something about themselves that they think is worthy of sharing with us, something that makes them unique, different, and the type of medical student and future physician that we're all looking for. What have they done in working with individuals—whether it's serving as a checker or bagger at a grocery store or working with handicapped individuals or tutoring inner-city kids—that shows they can relate to people and have they done it in an effective fashion? What the applicant should do in all respects is to depict why he or she is a unique individual and should be sought after. Of course, if they start every sentence on a whole page with "I," it gets to be a little bit too much.

A rare applicant doesn't use the space at all and I think that's a mistake—to leave the page blank. Here's an opportunity to tell something personal about themselves and separate themselves from, in our case, thousands of other applicants. So if the applicant doesn't use the space, I think that's certainly an error. An occasional applicant jots down something that isn't carefully thought through or even proofread for spelling or grammatical errors. In medicine we want reasonably compulsive individuals (although they should not be excessively compulsive) who are going to be careful and accurate in all their dealings, the type of person to whom we'd want to go when we're ill, someone who's going to pay attention to details and have things done correctly. Some people are going to place more emphasis on those small details than others, but I think it tells you something about the applicant and his or her approach to life and to responsibilities.

Lili Fobert
Admissions Officer
UCLA School of Medicine

You do look for motivation because the Personal Comments (section) is the only place the applicants have to indicate this. In other words, why are they interested in medicine? I don't think there's anything else specifically that we look for, other than whatever the applicant wants to tell about himself or herself.

The essay is read at UCLA by our screening committee, which is composed of about 25 people. Of course, each essay may not necessarily be read by every person on the committee.

Other Selected Graduate Programs

Ruth Miller
Former Director of Graduate Admissions
The Woodrow Wilson School of Public and International Affairs
  (Princeton University)

It's possible to redeem yourself (in certain cases) or to kill your chances of admission with the personal statement. What's most important to me is for the candidate to make a compelling case for himself or herself. I want to be persuaded that I should admit this person. Good writing is important in this regard. Secondly, I look for the person's sense of what our program is all about and why it makes sense in terms of his or her career plans. We ask for two essays. One is a personal statement of motivation—why you want to come. It's supposed to be about 1,000 words (as is the public policy memorandum we also require). I want to get a sense of what the applicant is all about. First, they should tell me where they're coming from—what it is in their background that leads them to apply to a program like ours. Second, they should tell me what it is they want to get out of our program. Third, I want to know where they hope our program will eventually take them in their career. We want to get a sense of the person's commitment to the world of public affairs, whether they're interested in housing in the inner city or development in the Third World. It's important for us to know that an applicant is not simply motivated by making large sums of money. They may end up doing that, but we want to see some kind of commitment to making the world a better place. Now that's a really corny thing to say, but that is the underlying philosophy.

"I was a foreign service brat and grew up all over the world and that's what made me interested in international affairs" might be part of the personal part of someone's essay. But I don't need to know about their relationship with their brother. (There are cases, though, for which the applicant's personal life has a very direct bearing on why he or she wants to come to the Woodrow Wilson School.)

There are two common mistakes applicants make. An applicant will do a standard essay for half a dozen schools on a word processor and adapt it slightly for each school. But then one may forget to change one of the school names. There is nothing more irritating than reading a long essay that concludes with "And that's why I want to go to the Kennedy School at Harvard"—and you're sitting here on the Woodrow Wilson School admissions committee! The other mistake people make is talking about something they know nothing about. They'll say, "I want to do something in international relations," without indicating that they have any idea of what that means. Or, "I want to go and cure the problems in the Middle East" or, "I want to go and work for the United Nations"—those kinds of grandiose statements that indicate to me that the person really doesn't know the realities of career opportunities in this field; they might just as well tell me they want to be Secretary General of the United Nations. This is a very common mistake and the younger the applicant, the more likely he or she is to make it. I also don't like to get a sense that the applicant has dashed off the statement in 20 minutes and hasn't given much thought to it. Ours is a very, very competitive admissions situation—we get about 600 applications and make only about 80 offers of admission—and the personal essay is the one opportunity to tell the admissions committee why you want to come and why we should accept you over the next person who is equally well qualified academically. You have to distinguish yourself in some way. And you really have to let the admissions committee know what it is about this program in particular that interests you. For example, you could mention that you like that there is a small core of required analytical courses here at the Woodrow Wilson School and that then you're free to select a field of concentration and build up a substantive background in that field. Now if I read something like that, I would know that the applicant had read our catalog and understood what our curriculum was about and what was distinctive about our program. You need to write well, and check grammar, spelling, and punctuation. You also definitely need to type or do the application on a word processor. The days of handwritten career statements are over. The only way I would even want to accept something like that would be if the applicant is in the Peace Corps in Zaire and doesn't have access to a typewriter or word processor. But I get very annoyed with a handwritten career statement in any other circumstance. Also, avoid cuteness; we've had people who have done career statements in the form of a miniplay, for example. You want to sound like a professional, even though we know you're not in many cases. It's a really different process from applying to undergraduate college. You don't want to sound naive; that doesn't mean you don't want to sound *idealistic,* because many of the people who write to us impress us with their commitment and sense of dedication.

As director of graduate admissions, I read all of the statements, and I screen out about half of them. One other person reads those I've screened out just to double-check me. So the applicant's file may be read by as few as 2 people. If you are admitted, your file will have been read by a minimum of 6 people and could be read by as many as 14 (everyone on the admissions committee).

Professor H. A. Kelly
Vice Chairman of Graduate Studies / English
UCLA

The applicants are warned to make the personal statement a good one because it will be regarded somewhat as a writing sample. We look for intelligence, lack of naiveté, determination to do well, solid reasons for wanting to go into the profession, realistic assessment of what one can do with a Ph.D. in English, and so on. If there are deficiencies in the numbers on the grade point average and on the Graduate Record Exam, then the personal statements are read for explanations of the low grades or scores.

If there are mistakes in proofreading—in spelling and so forth—that is a very bad sign. If there are mistakes in the sort of literary history that is brought to bear—for example, if someone's favorite author is John Milton and he or she says things that really aren't very impressive or that are untrue about Milton, then those things are held against the student. On the other hand, if the applicants show themselves to be right at home over a certain range of literature—in describing the sort of things they've had in the past and the specialties they'd be interested in in the future—that's chalked up to their credit.

Don't be literary or flowery. Be straightforward, business-like, hard-headed rather than overly sentimental—the simpler, the better. The statement should normally be neatly typed and not handwritten. Handwriting gives an impression of haste and casualness, offhandedness. Also, if the statement is presented on a separate sheet—rather than on the space provided—that always looks a bit more impressive, I think. We get a lot of people who get into the profession because they love literature and they are budding poets themselves; that doesn't necessarily bode well for success in our program, which is not on the creative side but rather on the research side. So too much stress upon one's desire to get a Ph.D. so that one will be able to compose better poetry really isn't very impressive. We don't have a Master in Fine Arts; we're more for teachers and research scholars.

We have a screening committee of 3 people who read the statements; later on, the whole graduate committee, which would be 4 more people, might look at it when we're handing out fellowships and making final decisions on admissions.

Professor Slobodan Ćuk
Chairman, Admissions Committee for Electrical Engineering
California Institute of Technology

We're not really looking for a biography but more for an explanation of why they have chosen Cal Tech and what they want to do in the future. They should give us some impression of what they're good at, their area of interest, and what they want to specialize in. Being a relatively small school that excels in the areas that it attacks, Cal Tech would like to match the faculty with the students, so it's very important to find out that there is some corresponding research field being actively pursued here at Cal Tech that the student is interested in. Typically, students write one to two pages, but sometimes we get extremes like ten pages or two sentences. Two pages is really what we consider optimum. We like to find out what's unique about the applicants by having that pointed out in the statements. These statements are read with very much interest because they give us some sense of the person behind them. We're also interested in why the applicants think they should receive their training at Cal Tech and not at other schools. We like honesty in the writing—if the statement comes out of the applicant's deep feelings, if it's really very personal, we can see that.

Mistakes? One applicant wrote that he'd like to be a Nobel laureate, so sometimes applicants have kind of exaggerated, unrealistic objectives. Sometimes they just list their extracurriculars when what we want is to see where they're heading. The other mistake is if the statement is too long. It becomes very difficult for a committee to read a five-page statement of objectives in which the applicant rambles on rather than focusing on what's most important. So if it's too long, too detailed, or too off the main course, this really turns off the committee. If the applicants spend enough time thinking about it, they will be able to focus on something unique that will be interesting for us to read.

The applicants should think about themselves and bring out as honestly as possible their real objective. Sometimes, through this statement, we can see the person who is more focused, more creative.

We have a committee of 5 people who are reading all these applications. For two months, we're buried in personal statements.

Professor Paul Green
Director, Master's Degree Program
Department of Biological Sciences (Stanford University)

We look for some research experience and some ability to assign proper values to various kinds of activities. In other words, can they distinguish important problems from trivial problems? We don't care particularly what they've done, but they should provide some evidence of judgment. They need to have some sense of proportion about the structure of the scientific community, the academic community, or the industrial/commercial community (depending on just what their ambitions are). We look for students who wish to make fundamental contributions. They usually say what they've done and what they would like to do, and we read both parts carefully. I think there's a full page provided in the form, but they're free to add other pages and they often do. We check to what extent the statement corresponds with letters of recommendation because often applicants will talk about their work and we'll have a letter from the person under whom they did the work.

I would say it's a mistake to fill up that page with details of the buffers they used in order to extract the rat liver; they should display a sense of proportion, they should know that we don't care what the concentration of calcium chloride was, and so on. Anybody with any judgment would realize that's a waste of our time. Often they praise the institution—referring to our "outstanding" this and "outstanding" that—and this is pretty much a useless exercise. If the statements are vacuous and full of platitudes, that's obviously a negative. If they can't be explicit about future plans, they should at least give some example of the kind of thing they consider important.

As they look back on their past, the applicants should extract the value of their efforts. In some cases, the efforts might not have been successful but the applicant can, above all, be honest and say "We tried this project; it didn't work and we learned why. Nonetheless, I like to do science, etc. . . ." It's just as effective to read an intelligent analysis of something that didn't work as a recital of a lot of things that did. It is the analytical capability that counts. And the same for future plans, as I indicated before; there should be some sense of proportion about what counts and a realization that you have to balance effort against reward: you want to maximize reward per unit of effort; some sense of ability to do that is looked for. You should avoid being overly colorful or cute. Somebody wrote, "What I like doing most is people." Well, that sort of makes you (the admissions reader) ill. So I'd say don't be too cute, don't be too boring, and show some analytical, interpretive skills.

Three or 4 people read each statement.

APPENDIX

On the following pages, you will find two separate, detachable questionnaires, one to hand out prior to writing your personal statement, the other to hand out afterward. These surveys will enable you to secure valuable input from friends, family, colleagues, professors, or others who know you. You can also benefit from carefully reviewing these questions and will find the second questionnaire to be an excellent means of assessing the worthiness of your initial effort.

PREPARATORY QUESTIONNAIRE

I am applying to _____
and must prepare a personal statement as a part of that process. I want to be sure to include all relevant data about myself and my background, so I am soliciting information from various individuals who know me and whose judgment I value. Thank you for your help.

1. What do you think is most important for the admissions committee to know about me?

2. What do you regard as most unusual, distinctive, unique, and/or impressive about me (based on our association)?

3. Are you aware of any events or experiences in my background that might be of particular interest to those considering my application to graduate school?

4. Are there any special qualities or skills that I possess that tend to make you think I would be successful in graduate school and/or the profession to which I aspire?

PREPARATORY QUESTIONNAIRE

I am applying to _____
and must prepare a personal statement as a part of that process. I want to be sure to include all relevant data about myself and my background, so I am soliciting information from various individuals who know me and whose judgment I value. Thank you for your help.

1. What do you think is most important for the admissions committee to know about me?

2. What do you regard as most unusual, distinctive, unique, and/or impressive about me (based on our association)?

3. Are you aware of any events or experiences in my background that might be of particular interest to those considering my application to graduate school?

4. Are there any special qualities or skills that I possess that tend to make you think I would be successful in graduate school and/or the profession to which I aspire?

PREPARATORY QUESTIONNAIRE

I am applying to _____
and must prepare a personal statement as a part of that process. I want to be sure to include all relevant data about myself and my background, so I am soliciting information from various individuals who know me and whose judgment I value. Thank you for your help.

1. What do you think is most important for the admissions committee to know about me?

2. What do you regard as most unusual, distinctive, unique, and/or impressive about me (based on our association)?

3. Are you aware of any events or experiences in my background that might be of particular interest to those considering my application to graduate school?

4. Are there any special qualities or skills that I possess that tend to make you think I would be successful in graduate school and/or the profession to which I aspire?

PREPARATORY QUESTIONNAIRE

I am applying to _____
and must prepare a personal statement as a part of that process. I want to be sure to include all relevant data about myself and my background, so I am soliciting information from various individuals who know me and whose judgment I value. Thank you for your help.

1. What do you think is most important for the admissions committee to know about me?

2. What do you regard as most unusual, distinctive, unique, and/or impressive about me (based on our association)?

3. Are you aware of any events or experiences in my background that might be of particular interest to those considering my application to graduate school?

4. Are there any special qualities or skills that I possess that tend to make you think I would be successful in graduate school and/or the profession to which I aspire?

EVALUATIVE QUESTIONNAIRE

I have composed the attached personal statement(s) for submission to
_____,
which I hope to attend. If you could take some time to read what I have
written and answer the following questions, I would be most grateful for the
benefit of your perspective.

1. Did my opening paragraph capture your attention?

2. Did you find the statement as a whole to be interesting?

3. Did you find it to be well written?

4. Did it seem positive, upbeat?

5. Did it sound like me?

6. Do you regard it as an honest and forthright presentation of who I am?

7. Did it seem to answer the question(s)?

8. Can you think of anything relevant that I might have inadvertently omitted?

9. Is there material within the statement that seems inappropriate?

10. Did you gain any insight about me from reading this?

11. Did you notice any typos or other errors?

12. Do you think the statement has in any way distinguished me from other applicants?

13. Do you think my application to _____is logical?

EVALUATIVE QUESTIONNAIRE

I have composed the attached personal statement(s) for submission to
_____,
which I hope to attend. If you could take some time to read what I have
written and answer the following questions, I would be most grateful for the
benefit of your perspective.

1. Did my opening paragraph capture your attention?

2. Did you find the statement as a whole to be interesting?

3. Did you find it to be well written?

4. Did it seem positive, upbeat?

5. Did it sound like me?

6. Do you regard it as an honest and forthright presentation of who I am?

7. Did it seem to answer the question(s)?

8. Can you think of anything relevant that I might have inadvertently omitted?

9. Is there material within the statement that seems inappropriate?

10. Did you gain any insight about me from reading this?

11. Did you notice any typos or other errors?

12. Do you think the statement has in any way distinguished me from other applicants?

13. Do you think my application to _____is logical?

EVALUATIVE QUESTIONNAIRE

I have composed the attached personal statement(s) for submission to

_____,
which I hope to attend. If you could take some time to read what I have
written and answer the following questions, I would be most grateful for the
benefit of your perspective.

1. Did my opening paragraph capture your attention?

2. Did you find the statement as a whole to be interesting?

3. Did you find it to be well written?

4. Did it seem positive, upbeat?

5. Did it sound like me?

6. Do you regard it as an honest and forthright presentation of who I am?

7. Did it seem to answer the question(s)?

8. Can you think of anything relevant that I might have inadvertently omitted?

9. Is there material within the statement that seems inappropriate?

10. Did you gain any insight about me from reading this?

11. Did you notice any typos or other errors?

12. Do you think the statement has in any way distinguished me from other applicants?

13. Do you think my application to _____is logical?

EVALUATIVE QUESTIONNAIRE

I have composed the attached personal statement(s) for submission to
_____,
which I hope to attend. If you could take some time to read what I have
written and answer the following questions, I would be most grateful for the
benefit of your perspective.

1. Did my opening paragraph capture your attention?

2. Did you find the statement as a whole to be interesting?

3. Did you find it to be well written?

4. Did it seem positive, upbeat?

5. Did it sound like me?

6. Do you regard it as an honest and forthright presentation of who I am?

7. Did it seem to answer the question(s)?

8. Can you think of anything relevant that I might have inadvertently omitted?

9. Is there material within the statement that seems inappropriate?

10. Did you gain any insight about me from reading this?

11. Did you notice any typos or other errors?

12. Do you think the statement has in any way distinguished me from other applicants?

13. Do you think my application to _____is logical?

About the Author

Richard J. Stelzer is a consultant who advises a wide array of clients on winning strategies for written presentations.

He is also an author with numerous journalistic credits. His first book, *The Star Treatment*, examined the personal problems and experiences in psychotherapy of 23 well-known personalities.

Mr. Stelzer was graduated from Vanderbilt University and holds a master's degree in journalism from the University of Missouri.

He has worked in both advertising and public relations and at one time served as a publicist for Dinah Shore. He lives in West Los Angeles, California.